The Woman Side of God

The Woman Side of God

by Dr. Connie Williams

End Time Wave Publications
Bogota, New Jersey

The Woman Side of God

ISBN 1-889389-16-1

Unless otherwise indicated, all Scripture quotations are from the King James Version of the Bible. Scripture quotations marked (NIV) are taken form the HOLY Bible, NEW INTERNATIONAL VERSION ®, Copyright © 1973, 1978, 1984 by International Bible Society. Used by permission of Zondervan Publishing House. The Amplified New Testament, Copyright © 1954, 1958, 1987 by The Lockman Foundation. Used by permission.

Those marked (NASB) are from the New American Standard Bible, Copyright © 1960, 1962, 1963, 1968, 1971, 1972, 1973, 1975, 1977 by The Lockman Foundation, La Habra, California. Used by permission.

Verses marked (TLB) are taken from The Living Bible, Copyright © 1971. Used by permission of Tyndale House Publishers, Inc., Wheaton, Ill. 60189.

Note: In some Scripture quotations, italics and quotation marks have been added by the author for emphasis only.

Typesetting: Sheila Chang
Cover: Mike Bennett (www.mikebennettgraphics.com)
Copy editor: Bob Juran

TABLE OF CONTENTS

DEDICATION

I dedicate this book to every woman who has ever felt Christ (the anointed One) move within her inward part (her spiritual womb) to establish a calling and ministry within her.

I trust that this book will cause that "babe" (ministry) to leap within you. I believe that this book is Truth and inspired by God. When Truth that is of God meets truth (the ministry) that is growing inside of you, the ministry will leap or be quickened, just as Truth leaped inside of Elisabeth when she met Mary carrying "the Truth."

> **And it came to pass, that, when Elisabeth heard the salutation of Mary, the babe leaped in her womb; and Elisabeth was filled with the Holy Ghost.**
> *Luke 1:41*

May those of you who thought your ministry was long dead be edified and encouraged so that the "babe" (the ministry) will leap, not die, but live, and declare the works of the Lord!

> **I shall not die, but live, and declare the works of the Lord.**
> *Psalm 118:17*

The inscription of my heart belongs to the four most important women in my life:

My grandmother, Fannie Lee Cannon, who is with the Lord in that great cloud of witnesses (*Hebrews 12:1* — Wherefore seeing we also are compassed about with so great a cloud of witnesses, let us lay aside every weight, and the sin which doth so easily beset us, and let us run with patience the race that is set before us). Her impartation of wisdom, life, and joy into my life has been my foundation.

My mother, Mattie Laura Cannon Price, without whom this book could never have been written. Thank you, Mom, for your support, your intercession, your understanding, your compassion, and your sense of humor. I love you very much and thank God for your influence in my life and ministry.

My mother-in-law, Alice Williams, who has continuously prayed for me and this ministry. God gave me "Granny A" as a gift! Thank you, mom-in-law, for your support! I love you!

And the most beautiful young lady in the world, my baby daughter, Daphne Aleena, has sacrificed her time with me since the age of 12 so that I might preach the Gospel. At the age of 9 she was the one who won me to the Lord! She is the most unselfish young lady that I know. Truly God ordained her into my life. How proud I am, Daphne, to be your Mother! I love you!

ACKNOWLEDGMENT

First of all let me acknowledge the Christ, the Revelation given, in Whom I live and breathe, and have my being.

Second, Perry Mallory, publisher of End Time Wave Publications, for his <u>tireless</u> work to get this book published. Perry is indeed one of my favored kingdom sons.

And to all those I know who sacrificed to send finances toward the publishing of this book.

> Bishop E. Bernard Jordan, Prophet Debra Jones
>   and Zoe Ministries
> Granny Matt (my mother)
> Rev. Mike Ruce (my brother)
> Kay Lenear
> Pastor Charles Mellette
> Dr. Charles Dixon
> Apostle Nell Matheson
> Attorney Robert Webb

To "<u>all</u>" those who labored with me financially and prayerfully. How faithful you have been to send finances and encouragement.

A special "thank you" to Evander and Janice Holyfield who "finished" this book for me— Evander and Janice, only God knows how your friendship has blessed me!! I love you!

To my dedicated and prayerful husband, Elder Curtis Williams, daughter Daphne A. Harris and son-in-law Mikey Harris, who have encouraged me to do all that is in my heart for the kingdom. My anointing has cost them a "normal" life and a normal wife, and a normal mother. They have paid a great price! May Father richly bless you my beloveds. You shall reap a hundred fold surely "in this life!"

To my "new" family, Michael and Sue Harris (Service Master, Woodstock, GA)

And lastly to the "loves of my life," my four nieces:
Jessica Underwood
Ashley Price
Heather Holyfield
Amy Laura Price, who <u>always</u> sows time, love and energy into <u>everything</u> I do!!

PREFACE

January of nineteen hundred eighty-three, when I became born-again, I immediately wanted to know everything about my Savior. Having known Him through denominations, through what people had shared with me, attending different churches, hearing different teachings and man's understanding, I came to realize that everyone had different opinions about Jesus. Some opinions were scriptural and some were not. I began to realize that there was a difference between opinion and "truth."

> **But the "natural" man receiveth not the things of the "Spirit" of God: for they are foolishness unto him: neither can he know** *them*, **because they are spiritually discerned.**
> *I Corinthians 2:14*

I was young in the Lord and just hungry for Him! All of Him! In October of nineteen hundred eighty-three, I received the baptism of the Holy Spirit. In nineteen hundred eighty-four, I began to feel the call to the ministry. On July 19, nineteen hundred eighty-four, I accepted that call. For three years I searched the Scriptures. I prayed and came out of my house only to fulfill the needs of my family and to attend church.

My family thought I was losing my mind. But what they did not realize was that I was discovering Christ as I had never seen Him before!

> **For every one that asketh receiveth; and he that seeketh findeth; and to him that knocketh it shall be opened.**
> *Matthew 7:8*

Out of my naivete, I believed that everyone would be happy for me leaving my old lifestyle to preach the glorious gospel of Christ and His Kingdom. It just didn't happen that way.

What I began to experience was neither happiness nor joy at God anointing me for ministry. There was no joy for the miracles, no joy for the healings, no joy for souls coming to the Kingdom, no joy for the life changes, no joy for the Word of the Lord being taught, and I began to experience persecution for being a woman winning souls to the Kingdom of Heaven.

How sad it was for me to see people who were born-again before me begin to persecute me for accepting God's divine purpose for my life. In those days, *Romans 8:28* became a reality and a promise to me personally.

> **And we know that "all" things work together for good to them that love God, to them who are the called according to "His" purpose.**
>
> *Romans 8:28*

I realized because God called me to "His" purpose and not my own, that "He" would somehow work even the bad things together for my good. But I will let you know this: Through the good, the bad, and the ugly, I began to seek the face of God as never before! I often wonder, since the Church so strongly stands against abortion in the natural, how many women carrying the anointing and God-given ministry of Christ have had spiritual abortions performed on them. Church, hear me with your spiritual ears! I will prophesy that the time is come that judgment must begin at the house of God! (*I Peter 4:17*)

For the time is *come* that judgment must begin at the house of God: and if it "<u>first</u>" *begin* at us, what shall the end *be* of them that obey not the gospel of God?
I Peter 4:17

You have Christians "saving the whales, saving the dolphins and saving mother Earth," and "saving unborn babies," but what about ministries? Before natural abortions on the world's women are judged, the spiritual abortions performed on God's women will be judged. Hear ye the Word of the Lord!

He that hath an ear, let him hear what, "not man," the Spirit saith unto the churches.
Revelation 2:7

It seems that someone in the Church could have laid down "man's" doctrines and refused to allow the religious instruments of men to "abort" that holy ministry that God had imparted into my inward part. They did not! So I give all the praise and the glory and the honor to Him for the revelation He reveals to me. Thank God for my Heavenly Father!

Since I was, and still am, so hungry to know Him, I constantly seek to know His "Whole Word." I seek Him for REVELATION, not EXPLANATIONS of the Scripture! In *I Corinthians 2:9* and *10*, Paul is telling the Christians at Corinth about the "hidden wisdom" of God that does not come by natural abilities.

But as it is written, Eye hath not seen, nor ear heard, neither have entered into the heart of man, the things which God hath prepared for them that love him.
I Corinthians 2:9

But God hath revealed them unto us by his "Spirit": for the Spirit searcheth all things, yea, the deep things of God.

I Corinthians 2:10

We must understand that we cannot, under any circumstances, know the deep things of God but by His Spirit. The following is the result of that search. The chronicles of the hours, days, months and years on my face before Him are resting in your hands.

I trust that this book will be a blessing to the Body. But most of all, it will also open the eyes and heart of the Church to what God is saying in this day and hour to His people.

Surely the Lord will do nothing, but he revealeth his secret unto his servants the prophets.

The lion hath roared, who will not fear? the Lord God hath spoken, who can but prophesy?

Amos 3:7,8

I write this book in humbleness, believing that His mercy and compassion will season every word and minister to every heart. I love God's people more than life itself, and it is my sincere desire that God reveal Himself and glorify Himself through this writing.

May the Lord anoint our eyes with eyesalve (*Revelation 3:18*), cause us to have an understanding heart (*Job 38:36*), cause our ear to hear (*Psalms 10:17*) and keep us established in not yesterday's moves and glory, but in this very hour's present truth (*II Peter 1:12*).

Dr. Connie Williams
June 1998

CHAPTER ONE

"REVELATION" OR "EXPLANATIONS?"

Actually, the Bible says, "Let the women keep 'SILENCE' in the Church."

There has been much debate over a woman's place in ministry. Some are quick to quote, "Keep a woman silent in church."

> Let your women keep silence in the churches: for it is not permitted unto them to speak; but *they are commanded* to be under obedience, as also saith the law.
> *I Corinthians 14:34*

There are people who want to take that Scripture literally, when it is convenient for "them."

For example, we have people in the Body who will quote that Scripture, but they will allow the women to teach Sunday school, to sing the Word of the Lord through music, to sing in the choir, to pray out loud, etc.

1

In fact, there are those who readily accept the intercessory prayers of women in church (and where would we be without our praying women?). Some have decided that they will twist the Word and call our women "missionaries" if they MUST be recognized. Some may say it is okay for a woman to sing, to teach Sunday school, or to pray!! Just don't preach!!

To that, my dear brothers and sisters, I say let us not distort or take the Word of God out of context. Let us not twist the Word to fit our own doctrines or beliefs. Let us take what is assumed to be the letter of the Word to the fullest, and not allow our women to speak at all; no conversation, no hellos, no prayer, no Sunday school teaching...nothing! Let us either "obey" the Word or not "obey" at all!

Or...we can make an intelligent decision to go to the Holy Spirit for a full understanding of God's Word. *John 16:12-15* declares that He is our Teacher and our guide into "ALL" truth.

I exhort the Church to stop trying to "explain" what we have not allowed the Holy Ghost to "reveal"! God would not have His people ignorant.

I know that the most popular excuse to dismiss Scripture concerning women is that our women in biblical days did not have the educational opportunities we have today. They were ignorant and spoke out of turn and interrupted services. So these familiar "women scriptures" were put in to keep order in the services. But I say these are all excuses, not revelation! With this in mind, who is right? What does the Word of God actually say? I would suggest, instead of going to man's carnal and egotistical understanding (*Proverbs 3:5*), we should go to the Holy Spirit. Either the Bible is "all" truth, or it is not! Let us not explain away any of the Scripture concerning women, but let us allow the Holy Spirit to anoint our eyes with eyesalve (*Revelation 3:18*) to fully understand what God is saying. We not only need to hear the Word of God, but we must also "see" the Word of God (*Isaiah 6:9*). Let us go to the One who inspired men to write the Bible (*II Peter 1:21*), and find out what He meant when He said certain things. Let us not lean to our own understanding. In all our ways, let us diligently and soberly acknowledge Him (*Proverbs 3:5 & 6*), and not attempt to enthrone our own personal doctrines. Let Him be our direction through the beautiful Scripture. Let us remember that Jesus said, "The words that I speak unto you, they are "<u>spirit</u>," and they are life" (*John 6:63*). Let us study to show ourselves approved that we do not become ashamed (*II Timothy 2:15*) for having taught error (personal belief or doctrine) instead of the Truth (the Person of Christ).

It would appear that The Truth has not been taught in the Church, especially to our women. For when the Truth is known, it will "make" you free (*John 8:32*). I have never seen as many women in bondage over Scriptures. I have never seen so much debate over Scriptures as I am seeing today. If we knew the truth, we would be free from such silly contentions. My dearest brothers and sisters, people are dying every day, crises arise anew every day, and yet the Church, who should be the light and salt of the Earth, is arguing amongst itself over petty doctrines. Should women be ordained and allowed to preach, teach, hold positions in the Church? Should we not allow all the captives to be set free to do the Work of the

Lord? Or shall we pick and choose who can labor for the harvest?

> **Then saith he unto his disciples, "The harvest truly is plenteous, but the labourers are few;**
>
> **Pray ye therefore the Lord of the harvest, that he will send forth labourers into his harvest."**
>
> *Matthew 9:37-38*

Let us remember, this is "His Harvest" and "He" is sending forth the "laborers."

CHAPTER TWO

THE SEPARATION OF SOUL AND SPIRIT

> For the word of God is quick, and powerful, and sharper than any two-edged sword, piercing even to the dividing asunder of soul and spirit, and of the joints and marrow, and is a discerner of the thoughts and intents of the heart.
>
> Neither is there any creature that is not manifest in "His" sight: but all things are naked and opened unto the eyes of Him with whom we have to do.
>
> *Hebrews 4:12-13*

First, we need to establish a basic definition of the Word of God. Many people think that the Bible is the Word. The Bible is "Scripture," ordained by God, written by men as the Holy Spirit moved.

> For the prophecy came not in old time by the will of man: but holy men of God spake as they were moved by the Holy Ghost.
>
> *II Peter 1:21*

My Bible declares that "The Word" was made flesh and dwelt among us; The Word we are talking about here is Jesus Himself!

> **And the Word was made flesh, and dwelt among us, (and we beheld his glory, the glory as of the only begotten of the Father,) full of grace and truth.**
>
> *John 1:14*

We have often divided the Word of Truth incorrectly. We quote, "Faith comes by hearing and hearing by the Word," implying "the scripture," of God (*Romans 10:17*). Your hearing is not going to come by letters on a page, but it is going to come by Jesus, "The" Word! Faith comes by hearing, but your "hearing ability" comes by Jesus (the Word). You can try to open your own ears until you are blue in the face, but until you allow "The" Word, King Jesus, to open those ears, faith will not come. The Psalmist said in *Psalm 40:6*, "Sacrifice and offering thou didst not desire. Mine ears hast 'THOU' opened." The Psalmist also said there are people who have "ears" but they hear not (*Psalm 115:6*).

Faith comes by "hearing" and "hearing" comes "by" and "through" Jesus (The Word). Now, "The" Word, Jesus, is quick and powerful, and "He" is sharper than any two-edged sword, piercing even as to the dividing asunder of the soul and spirit, the joints and the marrow, and "He" (The Word) is the discerner of the thoughts and the intent of the heart. Neither is there any creature that is not manifest in "His" (The Word's) sight: "But all things are naked and opened unto the eyes of Him (The Word) with Whom we have to do" (*Hebrews 4:12, 13*).

Jesus, the Word of God, is going to separate your soulish realm from your spiritual realm. Your spirit is what is tuned in and turned on to God. Since you live on this Earth, you have that soulish part, that mind, that will, that emotion, that "natural" man, which is contrary to God. You are, without divine intervention, driven by the demands of that soulish part of you that does not want to receive the things of God. The soulish, natural man does not want to know the things of God.

> **But the natural man receiveth not the things of the Spirit of God: for they are foolishness unto him: neither can he know them, because they are spiritually discerned.**
>
> *I Corinthians 2:14*

We know that the Word of God, who is Jesus, will divide the soul from the spirit. Jesus will open your ears so that you can know Him and hear His Voice. Contrary to popular belief, you can <u>know</u> if it is God or the devil, or your own mind that is speaking to you. When you allow Him, Jesus will divide your soul from your spirit. Then you can look at yourself and the decisions you are making and you can know when it's God's will or your will! When you allow "Him" to divide your soul from your spirit, you can be led by the Spirit and you will not lean and depend on your soul or your own understanding.

> **Which hope we have as an anchor of the soul, both sure and steadfast...**
>
> *Hebrews 6:19(a)*

Hope literally anchors the soul, which must be anchored and kept under subjection. There are times when the soul must be kept quiet. It is very important to discern between activity of the soul (referring to our mind, will and emotions) and the spirit (referring to Jesus within).

> **And the Lord God caused a deep sleep to fall upon Adam, and he slept: and he took one of his ribs, and closed up the flesh instead thereof;**
>
> **And the rib, which the Lord God had taken from man, made he a woman (wombed man), and brought her unto the man.**
>
> **And Adam said, This is now bone of my bones, and flesh of my flesh: she shall be called Woman, because she was taken out of Man.**
>
> **Therefore shall a man leave his father and his mother, and shall cleave unto his wife: and they shall be one flesh.**
> *Genesis 2:21-24*

We know that because Adam came from God, Adam was perfect. But Eve came from man. Eve was not perfect. God gave man His "Name" (meaning His nature), but man gave woman her "name" (and, in turn, her nature) (see *Genesis 2:23*).

What happens when you name something? You give whatever you name its NATURE! That is why Jacob was left ALONE and wrestled with a MAN—HIMSELF! (*Genesis 32:24*). His thigh (the place of reproduction) had to be touched in order to produce a different quality of life. The recognition of divinity within demands a change of nature and brings a change in reproduction. His name had to be changed from Jacob (which meant "supplanter") to Israel (which meant "He shall rule as God"), thus causing his NATURE to change, which caused Jacob (now Israel) to walk with a halt, or to walk differently from other men (*Genesis 32:31*).

8

There are three parts to "every" Christian: (1) spirit, which is the (Bridegroom Jesus) part; (2) soul, which is the woman (Bride Church) part; and (3) body, which is your natural flesh part.

And Jacob was left alone; and there wrestled a man with him until the breaking of the day.
Genesis 32:24

We have been in prison, in bondage to ourselves, wrestling with ourselves. Verse 24 tells us that Jacob was left "alone." But we are not going to win. There is going to be an impartation. There is going to be a changing of our name and our nature.

And when he saw that he prevailed not against him, he touched the hollow of his thigh; and the hollow of Jacob's thigh was out of joint, as he wrestled with him.

And he said, Thy name shall be called no more Jacob, but Israel: for as a prince hast thou power with God and with men, and hast prevailed.
Genesis 32:25-28

When we submit our will to God's will, we become one with Him. Jacob was the old realm and the old nature. The name of something or someone represents an imputed character, nature, and likeness. Our character, or our nature, has to be "formed" by God. He is in the process of changing our name, and He is changing our character. He is changing our likeness to that of Israel so that we, too, can rule as God in the earth.

God said, in *Isaiah 43:1*: **I "created" Jacob, but I am going to "form" Israel.** He is indeed giving us a "new name" **that at the name of "Jesus" every knee should bow, of things in heaven, and things in earth, and things under the earth (*Phillippians 2:10*).** Now, we come in the name of the Lord! Now we understand the Scripture in *Matthew 18:20*.

> **Where two or three are gathered together in "His" Name (nature), (not our own) He will be in the midst of us.**

Hopefully, we are casting out devils by not only "using" His Name, but by standing "in" His Name or Nature! *Mark 16:17*: **We shall be casting out devils not only through the power of that Name, but through the very Nature** (or compassion) **of that Name. Should not we do all things in His Name** (nature)? **Should not we ask all things in His Name** (nature), **so we do not ask amiss?**

> **Ye ask, and receive not, because ye ask amiss (with wrong motives and desires or in the wrong "nature"), that ye may consume it upon "your" lusts.**
>
> *James 4:3*

You may be going through a wrestling time with your old nature. But there is about to be an impartation, a touch to your thigh, because your loins (your thighs) must reproduce truth (after the spirit). Your loins may be reproducing after the soul, the woman. It may be hollow or empty, until there is an impartation. I can prophesy to you, "God is about to touch the reproducing part of the Body, and the Body is going to begin to walk with a limp." Everyone else is going to think it is "unnatural." What is unnatural to the world is natural to God.

The problem with the Church is that she has been walking just like the world. But when God begins to touch where we reproduce, and the power of God infuses our loins, we will begin to wrestle with the old man until our name, our character, our image and our very nature is changed into the image of God! We are a blessed people!

The Bible also lets us know that "Jacob" could not have seen God and lived.

> **And he said, Thou canst not see my face: for there shall no man see me, and live.**
>
> *Exodus 33:20*

To put it plainly and simply, "Jacob" had to die so that Israel could live!

The Bible says that when Israel left, he walked with a halt and passed over "the face of God" (Penuel). That old man could never see God and live! Jacob had been transformed into Israel.

> **But now thus saith the Lord that created thee, O Jacob, and he that formed thee, O Israel, Fear not: for I have "redeemed" thee, I have called thee by thy name; thou art mine.**
>
> *Isaiah 43:1*

> **And, behold, the angel of the Lord came upon him, and a light shined in the prison: and he smote Peter on the side, and "raised him up," saying, Arise up quickly. ("Gird thyself!" In other words, he told Peter, "Re-dress yourself! We are leaving this prison!") ....**
>
> *Acts 12:7*

My dear brothers and sisters, if you allow yourselves to be smitten, then you can be raised up! And if you are raised up, no prison can hold you! I like what Paul said: "I knew a man in Christ above fourteen years ago (whether in the body, I cannot tell; or whether out of the body, I cannot tell: God knoweth), such as one caught up to the third heaven (*II Corinthians 12:2*).

> **"Paul was raised up "and" caught up. He heard unspeakable words. He was caught up "into" paradise. He heard words, "not lawful for a man to utter."**
> **(*II Corinthians 12:4*)**

Can I tell you what the Church needs? The Church needs someone to come forth who has been caught up "into" God. The Church needs someone to come forth who has been caught up into His intelligence, caught up into His likeness and nature, and caught up into His Spirit. Someone needs to tell us some things that "man" cannot utter! Someone needs to tell us things that only the Holy Ghost can speak! That is what we desperately need! Man's words can never give us what we really need, which is life, and that more abundantly.

The angel smote Peter on his side and raised him up. If you will let yourself be smitten on your side, Jesus will raise you up. He will say, "Arise quickly," and your chains will fall off just as Peter's did (*Acts 12:7*). Then, as you come out of your prison, the angel will tell you to "gird thyself and bind on thy sandals" (*Acts 12:8*). We must have our loins "girt" about with truth and our feet shod with the preparation of the gospel of peace *(Ephesians 6:14-15)* if we want to leave the prison!

12

And he went out, and followed him; and wist not that it was true which was done by the angel; but thought he saw a vision.

When they were past the first (the flesh) and the second (the soul) ward, they came unto the iron gate that leadeth unto the city; which opened to them of his own accord: and they went out, and passed on through one street; and forthwith the angel departed from him.

And when Peter come to himself, he said, Now I know of a surety, that the Lord hath sent his angel, and hath delivered me out of the hand of Herod, and from all the expectation of the people of the Jews.

Acts 12:9-11

What the Church needs is a smiting on the side. We need to go past the first and the second ward, past the flesh and soul, past religion and our own ideas, past the first and the second thief, past the old man and the old nature, and go out of prison and into liberty! The chains need to be loosed off our hands so that we might labor in the vineyard, and we need to come out of prison and come into the city of God. We need to come to ourselves! We need to arise and return to our Father's house!

And when he "came to himself," he said, "How many hired servants of my father's have bread enough and to spare, and I perish with hunger!

I will arise and go to my father, and will say unto him, Father, I have sinned against heaven, and before thee."

Luke 15:17-18

Eventually, we will realize that we are living way beneath our privileges. We'll understand that our inheritance has been squandered. Our memory will come back, and we'll remember who and Whose we really are!

CHAPTER THREE

MAN HAS A WOMAN IN HIM

Genesis 5:1-2 declares:
This is the book of the generations of Adam. In the day that God created man, in the likeness of God made He him;

Male and female created He them; and blessed them, and called "their" name Adam in the day when they were created.

God took Eve from Adam. He caused a deep sleep to fall upon him and He took the rib that was in Adam and brought it outside Adam and formed Eve out of that bone.

I want you to see this with the eyes of your spirit, because I'm about to break the bonds of traditional thought that have blinded you to the truth. Did you not know that Eve was "in" Adam before she could be taken out? She was "in" Adam (*Genesis 2:21-22*), but God decided to take her out and make her separate from Adam. The moment Eve began to "operate," or "move" or "think" separately from Adam, she caused division in the garden. As long as Eve was inside

Adam, she was in obedience or in complete agreement with him.

Now, someone may say, "Adam was just one man." That is not what the Bible states. *Genesis* states, "They were created 'in' Adam, male and female, and He called them Adam."

Now, God chose to separate the man from the wombed man (or the woman). There is still a man part and a woman part inside each of us. There is a man and woman part in my handsome husband, Curtis. He is a man on the outside but on the "inside" there is also a man part and a woman part. That is why we are ALL called the bride (the woman, the wife) of Christ. We are all the woman part of Jesus, or the bride part, and Jesus is the male (or Spirit) part.

Adam and Eve were both in Adam. God took the rib part and He separated Eve out of Adam so that she might be separate. That is what happened to us. God took the rib from Adam's side and made him a wife, Eve. Adam said that Eve was bone of "his" bone and flesh of "his" flesh. God took the blood and water from Jesus' side and made Him a wife, the Body of Christ. We are now bone of His bone, and flesh of His flesh. We are now bone with Him; joined to Him as one. We are now led by Him, rather than being led by our flesh. If we are not baptized into Him, refusing the process of joining, and if we operate separately from Him, we will be just like Eve; we will always corrupt ourselves and eat from the tree of the knowledge of good and evil. In other words, we will feed ourselves what is pleasing to the eyes of our soul rather than allow Him to feed us the food of the Spirit.

Now we understand how we've adopted many of our patterns and habits of eating. In the natural, we eat what we want, what looks good to us, what sounds good to us, and what seems pleasant to us (*Genesis 3:6*), rather than eating from His table (*Psalm 23*). We prepare our own food, and we are in controversy with the truth that is from God. And this carries over into the realm of the Spirit. We pick and choose doctrines, concepts and ministries through the same demands of the soul—what looks good, sounds good and seems pleasant, rather than eating from the table of the Lord.

Eve was taken out of Adam and was made into a separate being. The man and the woman part, initially fused within Adam, were separated. The man part is subjected unto God, while the woman part is subjected or submissive to man and bears the responsibility of reproduction. When we see Jesus, we find that He, too, has a woman part and a man part. He is the Man, the Head, and the woman part is the Bride, or the Church, which is us. The Church is the body, the wife, the woman, the part that gives birth.

> **For ye remember, brethren, our labour and travail: for labouring night and day, because we would not be chargeable unto any of you, we preached unto you the gospel of God.**
>
> *I Thessalonians 2:9*

So we know that in Adam there was a man and a woman part. The man part, just as in Jesus, represents the spirit, and the woman (or the wombed part) always represents the soul.

Jesus, as the spirit, does well until the soul (which is us), the woman, moves separately from Him. Adam did all right as long as Eve was inside him, but when Eve was made separate, the first thing she did was to eat from the tree of knowledge of good and evil and, turning to Adam, she gave to him and he ate.

Eve ate because she was deceived (*Genesis 3:4*). Adam ate to cover Eve. The woman, or the soul, is the part that is always subject to deception. The Spirit can never be deceived. Jesus did not die because He sinned, for He was without sin. But He died because <u>we</u> sinned!

> **For he hath made him to be sin for us, who knew no sin; that we might be made the righteousness of God in him.**
> **   *II Corinthians 5:21***

Just as Adam covered Eve for her sin, so did Jesus cover His "Eve" (us) for our sin. Now we understand why Adam said, "Lord, the woman thou gavest me" (*Genesis 3:12*). Some people like to preach that Adam was pushing the blame on Eve. Not so! Adam was reminding God that He had given Eve to him in covenant, and therefore it was Adam's "responsibility" to cover Eve.

> **For this cause shall a man "leave" his father and mother, and shall be joined unto his wife, and they two shall be one flesh.**
> **   *Ephesians 5:31***

Adam wasn't casting blame, but accepting his responsibility to cover, for they two were one flesh.

THE FIG TREE IS CURSED

You are not made to walk in the soul, but to walk in the spirit. You were not designed to lean to your own foolish understanding; rather you are expected to acknowledge God, that Spirit part, and let Him direct your path (*Proverbs 3:5-6*). Your victory lies in not walking in the natural (soulish realm), but your overwhelming power is found when you walk in the supernatural!

We have all kinds of problems in our body because we are trying to live and walk in the natural, but we are spirit beings. We are trying to walk in the natural and we are supernatural. We are trying to walk in a place where we do not fit. Like Eve, we have allowed our soulish eyes to be opened.

When Adam and Eve realized that their soulish eyes were opened, they reached for fig leaves to cover themselves. For the first time, their soul was showing them the pain of shame, and they were exposed to the pain and turmoil of emotional disturbance generated by the soul. Like Adam and Eve, whenever we allow our soulish eyes to be opened, we take the fig leaves of religious rationale and attempt to cover ourselves, too! That is why Jesus cursed the fig tree in *Matthew 21:19*. He will never again allow us to cover ourselves! We are to be naked before Him until we are clothed with that which is from heaven.

For we know that if our earthly house of this tabernacle were dissolved, we have a building of God, an house not made with hands, eternal in the heavens.

For in this we groan, earnestly desiring to be clothed upon with our house which is from heaven:

If so be that being clothed we shall not be found "naked."

For we that are in this tabernacle do groan, being burdened: not for that we would be *unclothed*, but *clothed* upon, that mortality might be swallowed up of life.
**   *II Corinthians 5:1-4***

In cursing the tree, Jesus said that no man would eat the fruit of that tree, which represents a false covering of religious doctrine and pretense.

You can become a "church member," you can sew your own apron, or you can do anything you want to with those leaves, but God will still find you. He will still see you and He will still rebuke you.

You can hide among the leaves in a vain attempt to get away from the sound of His Voice, but His Voice is going to walk right up on you, and until the Blood of Jesus washes you *(John 3:3)* and you are truly born again, you will not be covered after eating from that tree of religiosity, you will never really see the Kingdom of God in its reality.

Those who are separated, like Eve, are driven by the demands of a blinded soul. They are busy making themselves (or covering themselves) with aprons. The soulish part desires to eat from the tree of knowledge of good and evil. That is why the woman part, or the soul, has a problem; she is always seeking advice and cannot discern whether it is good or evil. She wants to eat from the tree of knowledge of good and evil rather than submit herself to the spirit part (the man) and embrace the ways of the Lord.

According to the Word of God, we see what God has to say about her wanting to come out from under the spirit covering and go grab a piece of fruit from the tree of knowledge of good and evil. She uncovers herself. She opens her soulish eyes, she begins to lean to her own understanding, and she begins to walk in the deception and delusion found in the natural. She steps out of faith and into fear, and she walks out from under the covering of her headship, her spirit man! Before she knows whether she does not even know if she is saved or not—nor does she care.

Our soul woman has to be anchored, subdued, submitted, and covered by the Spirit man of God. We have to realize that we cannot lean to our own understanding, but we must acknowledge Him (the man, the spirit) and let Him be the Director of our path.

We must refuse to be led by our soulish part (our woman part). She will always want to eat of the wrong tree. Jesus within, that spirit part of us, will cause us to eat of the Tree of Life, because He is the Tree of Life.

He that hath an ear, let him hear what the Spirit saith unto the churches; To him that overcometh will I give to eat of the tree of life, which is in the midst of the paradise of God.
Revelations 2:7

What did God do once the soulish part (Eve) fell and her eyes were opened? He did not want her to be that way eternally, nor could He let her eat from the Tree of Life in her fallen state. So He put cherubims to guard the tree with a flaming sword which turned every way so that Eve could not eat from the Tree of Life in a fallen state. Too many of us want to eat from the Tree of Life by utilizing our soulish part. We want to lean to our own understanding.

We want to figure out God through our soul. We want to see Him with our soulish eyes. We want to package God according to the appetite of our soul. God says we are not to lean to our own understanding, but we are to acknowledge Him because He is going to give us direction. God put the cherubims there, He put the flame there, and He put the sword there because before we can eat from the Tree of Life now we must go through "The Way" that is being kept.

> **So he drove out the man; and he placed at the east of the garden of Eden Cherubims, and a flaming sword which turned every way, to <u>keep the way</u> of the tree of life.**
> *Genesis 3:24*

We have to go through the fire and we have to go through the sword, which is the Word of God, Christ, "The Way" (John 14:16). There are no shortcuts! Most of us do not want to go through the fire, the sword, the purging and purifying, nor the TEST to get to the TESTimony! Our souls may drive us to say we really want to be used by God. Our souls may make us say that we really want the anointing manifested in our life, but how many of us are really willing to pay the price?

It grieves me when I hear someone say, "I want to be like television evangelist so-and-so, or like missionary so-and-so." They do not know the price those people had to pay. We have a price to pay for our own anointing, and for our own calling, and that price is not cheap!

> I counsel thee to "buy of me" gold tried in the fire, that thou mayest be rich; and white raiment, that thou mayest be clothed, and that the shame of thy "nakedness" do not appear; and anoint thine eyes with eyesalve, that thou mayest see.
>
> *Revelation 3:18*

There must be a decrease of you for there to be an increase of Him in your life (*John 3:30*). You will be called to make many sacrifices; your life can never be your own. You have been purchased (*I Corinthians 6:20*). God is free, but He isn't cheap! There is a price to pay to hear from God! There is a price to pay if you want to really "know" God intimately. There is a price to pay to taste of Him in His "fullness."

> That I may "know" Him, and the power of "His" resurrection, and the fellowship of "His" sufferings, being made comformable unto "His" death.
>
> *Philippians 3:10*

God made it that way. There is a sacrifice to "really" hear from Him. If you do not believe it, come hang around with me for a week or two. You do not believe there is a price to pay? Your "salvation" is "freely" given unto you, but Jesus had to pay for your salvation with His life. There is a price to walk in "His" glory, and you must consider the cost.

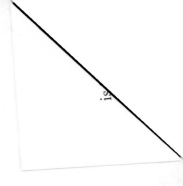

CHAPTER FOUR

THE SOUL IS A BRUTE BEAST

I am a spirit, I have a soul and I live in a body, and so do you! My spirit part, or man part, is Jesus (thank God), but my woman part, the bride part, is the soulish part. She, the soul, does not want to fast. She does not want to pray. She wants to eat from the tree of knowledge of good and evil and wants to feed it to the spirit or bring a mixture into this house (the body).

> **What? know ye not that your body is the temple of the Holy Ghost which is in you, which ye have of God, and ye are not your own?**
> *I Corinthians 6:19*

But if my woman is submitted to my husband, my man part, the spirit, I will not eat what I want to eat. I will eat only what He allows me to eat, so I will be covered by Him. When Adam and Eve were separated, Eve (woman) began to walk out of agreement with Adam (her man).

We see now that just as we have been separated from Jesus in times past, we, as His rib, are being joined back into Him. Now we understand why Adam's side was closed. God ʌnished with flesh. Jesus' side is not, because members are continuously being reconciled and restored back into Him.

As far as God is concerned, He is finished with the "earth man" (*I Corinthians 15*), but the last man is still being "assembled."

> **Not forsaking the assembling of ourselves together, as the manner of some is....**
> *Hebrews 10:25a*

So we see that it is not Jesus, the man, who is disobedient, but it is the bride, the woman, to whom He is joined. We are bone to His bone and flesh to His flesh. It is we, the woman, who caused the trouble. In *Genesis 3:1*, God declares that the serpent was more subtle than any beast of the field that He had made. Now if you want to know what a beast is, you must hear me by the Spirit. A beast is not cats and dogs, or cattle and things of that nature.

Jude 10 talks about men who turn to their own understanding and choose to know things "naturally" rather than by the "Spirit." They are described as "brute beasts."

> **But these speak evil of those things which they know not: but what they know <u>naturally</u>, as brute beasts, in those things they corrupt themselves.**
> *Jude 10*

> **But these, as natural brute beasts, made to be taken and destroyed, speak evil of the things that they understand not; and shall utterly perish in their own corruption.**
> *II Peter 2:12*

If you lean to your carnal understanding and you lean or depend on your own knowledge, that is a beast nature. It is unnatural, it is corrupt!

I said in mine heart concerning the estate of the sons of men, that God might manifest them, and that they might see that they themselves are "beasts".
Ecclesiastes 3:18

A beast has no covering. A beast is not submitted to the man part or Spirit of God. That is why, in the last days, there is going to come up a beast nature out of this earth (the carnal realm) or out of the first Adam. The first man "of" the earth, "earthly."

And I beheld another beast coming up out of the earth; and he had two horns like a lamb, and he spake as a dragon.
Revelations 13:11

I Corinthians 15:47 says the first man is of the earth; making him "earthy." He is going to want to make an image of himself. But praise be unto God! There is a different image that is being raised in our temple!

For whom he did foreknow, he also did predestinate to be conformed to the "image of his Son", that he might be the firstborn among many brethren.
Romans 8:29

The image or likeness of Christ! We are being conformed, not to the image of the beast, but to the image of Christ. We must refuse to bow down and worship or submit ourselves to our own desires, i.e., "my career," "my image," "my ministry," "my this," and "my that"! We will not lend our members to another.

Neither yield ye your members as instruments of unrighteousness unto sin: but yield yourselves unto God, as those that are alive from the dead, and your members as instruments of righteousness unto God.

Romans 6:13

I refuse to yield or bow to the image of a beast!

I speak after the manner of men because of the infirmity of your flesh: for as ye have yielded your members servants to uncleanness and to iniquity unto iniquity; even so now yield your members servants to righteousness unto holiness.

Romans 6:19

We will submit to our husband (Jesus) and He will cherish us! (*Genesis 3:1-4*) The Psalmist got a revelation of this in the Old Testament when he said (*Psalms 34:2*): **My soul shall make "HER" boast in the Lord. The humble shall hear thereof, and be glad.** The humble are glad when the "woman" (soul) makes her boast only "in" the Lord! The Lord said, "the serpent was more subtle than any beast of the field which the Lord God has made," and he said unto the woman, "yea, hath God said ye shall not eat of every tree of the garden?" And the woman said unto the serpent, "we may eat of the fruit of the trees in the garden: but of the fruit of the tree which is in the midst of the garden, God hath said: Ye shall not eat of it, neither shall you touch it, lest you die." And the serpent said unto the woman, "Ye shall not surely die."

It is of the nature of the devil to "distort" what God says! (Compare what God actually said in *Genesis 2:17* with what Eve repeated in *Genesis 3:3*). The serpent communicates with the woman, the soulish part. The devil does not come at your spirit (the male part).

He does not come at the Christ that dwells in you! The Spirit—the man—is the Christ in you. The devil comes to that woman part, that soulish part, to tempt her to eat of her own understanding. And the first thing the soul does is distort what God really said. God did not tell her she could not touch the tree; He just told her not to eat it.

The first thing the soulish part does is misunderstands what God has said. We must hear God by the Spirit and not by the soul (or by the flesh), or we will misunderstand Him. That is the problem that so often manifests with preachers. We hear by the flesh (soul), and not by the Spirit. The soul, the woman part, always adds to, or takes away from, what the Scripture actually says. The woman (the soul) wants to bring mixture into the body (God's temple). The serpent lied to the woman and told her, "You will not die."

> **For God doth know that in the day ye eat thereof, then your eyes shall be opened, and ye shall be as gods, knowing good and evil.**
>
> **And when the woman saw that the tree was good for food, and that it was pleasant to the eyes, and a tree to be desired to make one wise, she took of the fruit thereof, and did eat, and gave also unto her husband with her; and he did eat.**
>
> **And the "eyes" of them "both" were opened, and they knew that they were naked; and they sewed fig leaves together, and made themselves aprons.**
>
> ***Genesis 3:5-7***

Did you know God never wanted you to "see" by the soul?

He never wanted the woman's eyes opened! He only wanted us to see by the Spirit or by the man part of us! *II Corinthians 5:7* says: **"For we walk by faith, not by sight."**

When you eat from the tree of knowledge of good and evil, your soulish eyes will be opened, and you will see things your soul was never meant to see.

You were meant to see through the eyes of the spirit man. We understand why the Body of Christ is having heart attacks, nervous breakdowns, cholesterol problems, and other ailments. This can be attributed to walking in the natural. We were not "created" to walk in the natural. We are no longer equipped to walk in the soulish realm. We were created to walk in the Spirit. So when we try to walk in the natural, or by the soulish realm, when you begin to eat from the tree of knowledge of good and evil, our soulish eyes are opened.

> **But the natural man receiveth not the things of the Spirit of God; for they are foolishness unto him; neither can he know them, because they are "spiritually discerned".**
> *I Corinthians 2:14*

You will walk in fear, you will walk in doubt, your body will get sick and you will carry burdens of worry and oppression and depression. You are walking out of your place! You will begin to desire the wrong tree because it "looks" good to you. You were not created to use your soul to see, nor was your "soul" meant to make decisions for you!

CHAPTER FIVE

THE WOMAN SIDE OF JESUS

We know that the Bible is written in the language of God. It was inspired by the Holy Ghost, but we have taken our soulish part (our woman part), eaten from the tree of knowledge of good and evil, and tried to "figure" God out. We have said that female means "a woman with breasts." We've taken a natural definition and tried to conceptualize God according to the natural mind.

We have said a woman is a female and a man is a male, but God says, "There is neither Jew nor Greek, bond nor free, male nor female when you come 'into' Christ" (Galatians 3:28). So what does God mean by "woman"? He means that soulish part that is found within each of us! He's not referring to the gender of our physical bodies; He's talking about that part of us that is supposed to be under subjection to His Voice—to that part which is supposed to be covered by the spirit (the man part).

The soulish part (the woman part) is the part with a womb. We are Jesus' woman part. We are the part of Jesus that gives birth, regardless of whether you are a male or female in the natural. In the "spirit" you are the woman part of the Body of Christ. You are the bride; you are the great pearl that He loved so much, He sold all He had and bought you! (*Matthew 13:46*)

JESUS DIED FOR THE WOMAN

I like what Paul said in Ephesians 5:31:

For this cause shall a man leave his father and mother, and shall be joined unto his wife, and they two shall be one flesh.

We do not read past that, but if we did, in verse 32 he says,

This is a great "mystery": but I speak concerning Christ and the church,

If we are going to be part of Him and joined to Him, and be bone of His bone, and flesh of His flesh, we must sometimes leave what has produced or birthed us in the natural realm!

Paul tells us that he was separated from his mother's womb (*Galatians 1:15*). I don't know what you can describe as your "womb," but my womb was once a church where we could not wear lipstick or any kind of makeup or jewelry. I had to be separated from that womb, that soulish womb. I was eating from the wrong woman!

I had to be separated from that womb so that Christ could be "revealed" in me. Paul said that if a man would leave his father and his mother, and would cleave unto his wife, then they would be one flesh. Jesus said this was a mystery. The Bible is full of mysteries! (*I Corinthians 4:1*) But when Jesus was on the cross, He fulfilled that mystery!

> **When Jesus therefore saw His mother, and the disciple standing by, whom He loved, He saith unto His mother, Woman, behold thy son!**
>
> **Then saith He to the disciple, Behold thy mother! And from that hour, that disciple took her unto his own home**
> *John 19:26-27*

After this, Jesus knew that "all things" were now accomplished (*John 19:28*).

In Matthew's account of the crucifixion, in the 27th Chapter, the 46th Verse, Jesus says, "My God, my God, why hast thou forsaken me?" God forsook Him because a man "must" leave his mother (John 19:26-27) and his father (Matthew 27:46) and "must" cleave unto his wife, the Church, us, so that "they" can become one flesh. Jesus fulfilled one of the greatest mysteries of all, Christ and the Church. God took the rib from the first Adam's side and made him a wife, Eve. God took the blood and water from the last Adam's side, and made Him a wife, who is us, the Church.

> **But one of the soldiers with a spear pierced his side, and forthwith came there out blood and water.**
> *John 19:34*

Now we understand why the veil in the temple was rent (*Matthew 27:51*). The head (Christ) was in the Holy of Holies and the body (us) was outside. There was a veil (flesh) between Him and His Body. When Jesus said it is finished, the veil (the flesh) was rent (His side was opened) and the head and the body were joined (*Hebrews 10:20*).

Now we are one, and now "we" are bone of His bone, flesh of His flesh; no longer separated by a veil. Hallelujah! We are no longer separated by flesh! He forsook His father and His mother so that He could join unto you and me, His bride! We are indeed His "pearl of great price." He sold all He had, forsook all, left Heaven, left Father, left Mother, was made a little lower than the angels (*Hebrews 2:7*), that He might buy us! (*Matthew 13:46*)

We have been bought with a price (*I Corinthians 6:20*), and what a price He paid! He died to save the woman (the Church) and the woman (the soul). He died for the woman!

> **Who, when he had found one pearl of great price, went and sold all that he had, and bought it.**
> **Matthew 13:46**

> **For ye are bought with a price: therefore glorify God in your body, and in your spirit, which are God's.**
> **I Corinthians 6:20**

You are the part that gives birth. Did not Paul say "I" will travail in birth until Christ be formed in you? (*Galatians 4:19*) Did not *Isaiah 66:8* say that Zion (the Church) had to travail to bring or birth forth her children? We, the bride, are the woman part of Jesus. We are the part that brings forth sons and daughters into the kingdom of God.

We are the part that gives birth to the things of God. So we know that Jesus' meaning of a "woman" goes much deeper than our meaning. He implies much more than what the physical realm can employ. That is why the bride has two breasts; there is a soulish breast and there is a spiritual breast.

I do not know about you, but I nursed off that soulish breast for five years, and it did not nourish me. I was so malnourished and hungry for God with a hunger that could not be quenched, until God began to reveal the spiritual side of the breast. He began to give me that pure, sincere milk of the Word (*I Peter 2:2*). *Revelation 15:6* reveals to us that angels are coming forth. Divine "messengers" are coming forth out of the temple (Church) having their "breasts" girded with golden girdles.

There is a people coming forth out of the Church with their breasts girded about with gold, carrying a message of purity. These are a people that have been through the fire. And in their breast is the pure Word of God...unpolluted, undefiled, and unmixed. They are going to feed the <u>sons of God</u>, not with the doctrines of men, but with a pure Word from the man, Jesus Christ!

We are the breast of God. We can allow a hungry generation to taste and see that the Lord is good through what His breast (His bride, His woman part) can give. Being God's woman does not mean whether you have breasts or not in the natural, because whether you are a male or female in the natural, when you become joined to Him, you automatically become His bride, His woman. You become the woman part or the soulish part of Him.

We are now being brought back "into" Jesus. That rib is coming back to Jesus, and that blood and water *(John 19:34)* is coming back into the body. We are no longer separated from Him, but we are one with Him. We are covered by the spirit (part), covered by the man (part), covered by the head (part), and we are bone of His bone and flesh of His flesh, just like Eve was to her Adam.

> **And Adam said, This is now bone of my bones, and flesh of my flesh: she shall be called Woman, because she was "<u>taken out</u>" of Man.**
>
> *Genesis 2:23*

Whenever you hear someone talk to you out of their soulish part, you should say to them, "Unless you are covered by the Spirit of God (the man) eating from the Tree of Life, I do not want to hear anything you have to say." There are too many voices of the woman (the bride or the soulish part) speaking in the Church today!

The woman, the Church, should be silent and let the "Christ" <u>man</u> speak "through" Her!

> **But I suffer not a woman to teach, nor to usurp authority over the man, but to be in silence.**
>
> *I Timothy 2:12*

A lot of preachers may look like men and wear pants, but I still hear the woman's (soulish) voice—let he that hath an ear HEAR what the SPIRIT saith unto the Church!!

CHAPTER SIX

THE ENTICEMENTS OF THE SOUL

It is vitally important that you see and perceive what I am saying through your spiritual eyes! Any time God gives you a truth, you can check it from Genesis to Revelation. It will line up with the Word of God! Let us take this all the way through the Bible. Sarah, being the soul (woman) that she was, and Abraham, being the spirit (man) that he was, finally listened to God and birthed Isaac, the promise. But when he listened to the soulish part (meaning Sarah, the woman), the result was an Ishmael. (Weren't Sarah and Abraham married, making them one?)

When the soul operates separately from the spirit, she will bring forth an Ishmael (which means "a child by the flesh"). But when she operates from the spirit (the man) in cooperation with the Spirit of God, she will birth an Isaac (a child of promise or the promise of God as ordained by God). When an Abraham listens to a Sarah, he will end up in a tent with Hagar, producing after the soul because he listened to the soul (Sarah) instead of the Spirit (God). That is why Sarah could say, "My wrong be upon thee" (Genesis 16:5). The spirit never listens to the soul. The soul must submit to the spirit and listen to Him. The wife <u>must</u> submit to her husband!

The woman will always compromise. She will eat from the tree of knowledge of good and evil because it "looks good." Hagar seemed easier; she was "pleasant to the sight." Hagar met the standards of rationalization. Sarah had a problem believing God. She was seeing through the eyes of the soul. The woman (soul) lacks faith and will always take the easy way out.

You can look at Samson and Delilah in Judges 16:19. Samson (spirit part) laid his head in the lap of Delilah (the soulish part). The soulish Delilah would cause his eyes to be blind, his hair of his intelligence and glory to be cut off, and finally put Samson to sleep (thus losing his understanding and vision). He ended up working for the enemy. If you ever lay your head in the lap of the soul or depend on the soul, you too will lose your vision.

You can look at Hannah, who was barren until she went into the temple in I Samuel 1:10. She listened to what the man had to say. See, we are not designed to birth anything outside of the temple, or in other words, outside of the Church. We were not designed to birth anything outside of Abraham's household, or apart from our spiritual covering.

That is why the Bible says that if a woman shall put away her husband, she will commit adultery (*Mark 10:12*). Understand me by the Spirit! If you allow this woman part, this emotional part, to be joined to another man, or another "spirit," other than the Christ spirit, you will commit adultery.

The Bible says the woman (soul) is not to change the natural use of her body. Neither is the man (spirit) to lose the natural use of his body (*Romans 1:26 & 27*). The spirit is supposed to be the spirit, and the soul is supposed to be the soul. They each have their rightful place.

Neither is the woman (soul) supposed to put on the man's (spirit's) garment, nor the man (spirit) to put on the woman's (soul's) garment (*Deuteronomy 22:5*). Our problem is that we want to have a soulish church (a woman church) with all of our doctrines and programs and ideas that were spawned from the tree of knowledge of good and evil. But we want to dress her (the soul) up like the man (the spirit part) and call it God.

But God says you cannot dress the woman (soul) as the man (spirit); neither can you take the man (spirit) and dress him up with our soulish garments of religion. It is just not acceptable in the sight of God! I hope you can see this—the problem with the world is that it sees a TRANSVESTITE Church!! A woman (soulish organization) trying to dress itself with manly (spiritual) garments!!!

That is why we consistently find the woman (the soulish realm) at the well. Who is always thirsty (*John 4:7*)? The soulish part is ALWAYS thirsty!! People's souls are thirsty for the true Water of LIFE! That woman, the soul (remember that is the will and the emotions), is only looking for love! She is thirsty for her true Husband. I always say that there are a lot of woman (lost souls) at "Jacob's well," a watering place dug by our forefathers, drinking the water of a past message or move that still leaves us thirsty.

God bless them all, I love them, but beside a well "dug" by man, there is a living well <u>called</u> Jesus with Living Water!! If we will drink from that well, we will leave all those other husbands (doctrines, traditions, etc.), and all those other spirits we have been sleeping with and reproducing after, that are not God (*Jeremiah 17:13*). We will be joined to our <u>true</u> Husband! Then, and only then, will we never thirst again! He will be our only source of water (*John 4:13*). He and only He will feed us, and then we can stop running from one husband to another, looking for love in all the wrong places! We can stop our dance of futility and start a dance of fertility! He is Love! (*I John 4:8*). That is why the woman at the well (the soulish part) always has so many husbands until she meets THE husband. The soul is looking for her husband.

She must break or divide her own kingdom (*Mark 3:24-25*) of understanding and allow His understanding to come forth. She must acknowledge a higher understanding than her own (*Isaiah 55:8-9*). That is why the woman in Luke 7:37-39 (soulish part) brought the alabaster box to Jesus and began to wash His feet with tears and wiped them with the hairs of her head, kissed His feet and anointed them with ointment. Why do you think it was so important that the "woman" washed His feet? The woman (soul) takes "her" glory (*I Corinthians 11:15*) and yields her glory to the feet of Christ. When she does, the "whole house" (the Church) will be filled with the odor of the ointment. If only the whole Church would be "filled" with the odor of submission to Christ and submission to one another!

The woman (the soulish part) is "always" caught in adultery. Have you ever wondered why no one ever brings the man that was with the woman when she was caught? It is the soulish part that commits adultery. It is the soulish part that will join herself to other men ("forms" of Godliness) and have illegitimate babies. It is the soulish part that comes out from under the spirit of God and will listen to all kinds of things and go with whatever sounds good for the moment. She wants a quick fix for a soulish itch. She wants a lover, not a husband. She wants something that sounds good and tastes good and satisfies the "soul." Then she will lie with it and reproduce after its kind!

Now, hear me by the Spirit, please! This is why we have so many different doctrines. The woman (soul) would rather join herself to a "doctrine"— another spirit — rather than her husband — the true spirit — or Jesus the Christ.

I am thankful for *Mark*. He recorded Jesus saying, "If I drink any deadly thing, it shall not hurt me" (*Mark 16:18*). There is a serpent that is casting out water from his mouth (from his well) (*Revelation 12:15*), but I will not drink of it, not any more! I drank from that well for years, not knowing any better! But praise be unto God for *Mark 16:18*—IT DID NOT HURT ME!! It was deadly. Don't get me wrong. I drank of the poisonous religious doctrines of men, but it did not kill me!

If only the woman (soul) would discern whose "water" she is drinking! Water from the "living well" or water from the "serpent's mouth"!

And he saith unto them, Whosoever shall put away his wife, and marry another, committeth adultery against her.

And if a woman shall put away her husband, and be married to another, she committeth adultery.
Mark 10:11-12

Now if the woman (soul) doesn't return to her first love, Christ (spirit), she is committing adultery. Don't worry about your husband (Christ), Church!! He will never leave you nor forsake you (*Hebrews 13:5*). It's the woman (soul) that wants to put away the husband (spirit) so she can do whatever she wants to do! If the soul joins herself to any other spirit than the Christ (spirit), she commits adultery!

Your soulish part can be saved from bearing forth illegitimate children outside of the spirit, if you are walking in faith and love and holiness. For faith comes by hearing and hearing comes by The Word, the Jesus part, the spirit part. You will not birth after the soul and you will not birth after the natural. You will not birth Baptist babies, Methodist babies, Charismatic babies or any other denominational babies! We are to be joined to His Spirit! There are many spirits we can lie with and reproduce after; a spirit of religion, a spirit of jealousy, a spirit of the anti-Christ and so on and so on. But we're called to reproduce after the likeness of God!! We must produce "JESUS" babies! Let us quit kissing the wrong husband (spirit), who will only breathe the "wind of doctrine" into us. And let us begin to kiss our "true" husband, Christ. He will breathe into us the "breath of life." And then and only then will we become a "living soul"— woman.

CHAPTER SEVEN

LET THE WOMAN KEEP SILENCE

Let us make God's people free through Truth (John 8:32). Is that all right? I am talking soul and spirit, man and woman, created He them, and He called them both Adam (*Genesis 5:2*).

> **I will therefore that men (spirit) pray every where, lifting up holy hands, without wrath and doubting .**
> *I Timothy 2:8*

Who is supposed to pray? The man. What does the man represent? The Spirit! When you go to God in prayer, do not go to Him like He is the Holy Ghost Santa Claus. That is the woman (soul) praying. "God, Sister Smith got a new car. Let me have a new car, I want one bigger and brighter and better than Sister Smith's car." Shut up, woman! Shut up, soul! Shut up, "my" mind, "my" will and "my" emotions!

The man part, the spirit part, is supposed to do your praying so that you do not ask amiss that you may consume it upon "your" lusts (*James 4:3*). When you pray your "wants," you will become an adulterer (*James 4:4*).

In like manner also, that women adorn themselves in modest apparel, ("with Godly fear, and sobriety, not with braided hair").   *I Timothy 2:9a*

What did I tell you the hair represents? INTELLIGENCE!!! In other words, the Scripture is saying, "Do not work or lend your strength to your own understanding. Don't get caught up in twisted thinking. Do not work (or braid or twist) with the understanding that comes from the soul."

I am writing by the spirit; please understand me!

Gold, or pearls, or costly array; (let us not dress up the soul), But (which becometh women professing godliness) with good works.   *I Timothy 2:9b-10*

Do you know the best your soul can do? Good works.

But I suffer not a woman (soul) to teach nor to usurp authority over the man (spirit), but to be in silence.   *I Timothy 2:12*

Do you understand what God is saying? He is saying, "Soulish part, keep your mouth shut! We do not want to hear from you." Can I tell you that before I get behind the pulpit, I say, "Jesus, I command the woman, the soul in me, to be silent. I command that soulish realm to be silent. I command my natural understanding to cease. Because I want the man, the Spirit, to speak. I want to hear from the Spirit of the Living God!"

I want the man (spirit) to preach through me, not the woman (soul). I want Jesus to preach! The woman, the soul, needs to learn in subjection to her husband (or to her spirit). Let the woman learn in silence with all subjection.

But I suffer not a woman (soul) to teach nor to usurp authority over the man (spirit), but to be in silence.
I Timothy 2:12

Can I tell you most fearfully what is wrong with our churches? The woman (soul) is teaching and preaching behind our pulpits, on our television stations, in our schools, on the radios, and she is usurping authority over the man (spirit, the Christ). We need to put the woman in her place, under subjection to her husband!

For Adam was first formed, and then Eve (*I Timothy 2:13*). What is the Word talking about? Spirit and soul; Adam and Eve. I do not know if we realize it or not, but Adam was not deceived. **The woman** (the soul) **was deceived and was with transgression (*I Timothy 2:14*).** The spiritual part can never be deceived. That is why the serpent went to the soulish part, because even he is smart enough to know he could not have deceived the spirit part!

Notwithstanding she shall be saved in childbearing if "they" (soul & spirit) continue in faith and love and holiness with sobriety.
I Timothy 2:15

God wants to save us in childbearing and cause us to birth Jesus babies (Jesus Churches, the Jesus anointing, Jesus gifts, Jesus choirs, Jesus messages)! Would be that we would never birth anything "outside" of Him! If the woman continues in we would never birth anything "outside" of Him! If the woman continues in faith, love, and "holiness" (not adultery) with sobriety, praise God, the women can be saved! (*I Timothy 2:15*)

CHAPTER EIGHT

THE WOMAN, A TEMPLE PROSTITUTE

I pray that you ladies will stop letting anyone use the Scripture, "suffer not the woman to teach," to keep you from the purpose of God! There is neither male nor female "in" Christ (*Galatians 3:28*). There is a woman and there is a man, but there is no "male" nor "female." Hallelujah!

In *I Corinthians 11:3* it states, "But I would have you know, that the head of every man is Christ" (Who is the man? THE SPIRIT!). The head of the Spirit is Christ! Christ is also the head of the woman, who is the soul. The Head of Christ is God. Every man, every spirit, praying or prophesying, having his head covered, dishonors his head (*I Corinthians 11:4*).

Can I tell you that your spirit man does not need covering when he prays or prophesies? Your man part is Jesus, and He does not need a covering. He *is* the covering! But every woman, that soulish part, does! Every woman (that soul part) who prays or prophesies with her head uncovered (without being subjected to the Spirit), dishonors her head, for that is even all one as if she were shaven (*I Corinthians 11:5*).

This is so good! Your spirit part can pray or prophesy, but the soulish part, that woman part, if she is not covered by the spirit, she ought to keep her mouth shut! She needs to learn in silence to be subjected to her husband or bridegroom (*I Timothy 2:11*).

Do you know why? Because she will pray for new houses, new cars, designer outfits, new jewelry or whatever. Let him that hath an ear hear! She will always pray her own soul, her mind, her will, and her emotions, or her own desires, but not the spirit's. If you are praying your wants or your desires, you are praying without your head covered. You are not praying of your spirit, because the Spirit of God will not prompt you to pray such a thing. If the soul prays with her head uncovered, without the Spirit of God covering her, *James 4:2* says: **"You ask and receive not, because you ask amiss that ye may consume it upon 'your' lusts."**

You want to consume it upon your own lust, therefore you are praying through the soul and not by the spirit. You are praying uncovered. Your woman (soul, mind, your desire) is showing! Every woman who prays or prophesies with her head uncovered ought to be shaved (*I Corinthians 11:5*). What can I tell you about the woman who has her head shaved?

Well, first, what does it mean to be "shaved"? Remember that the hair represents intelligence. So a "shaved" head indicates a lack of intelligence and understanding. During the time and culture in which this was written, a woman who shaved her hair was indicating she was a prostitute. May I tell you that if you go and begin to prophesy or pray through the soul (the woman) without the spirit, you are prostituting the things of God? A woman (soul) can prophesy over you all day on Monday that you need to give her a hundred dollars; if you give her a hundred dollars, she can prophesy that Cadillac into your garage on Tuesday. A prostitute always charges, doesn't she? He that hath an ear, hear! They don't have to stick around to see if the Cadillac manifests on Tuesday.

So Prophet "Prostitute" will say, "I can see that Cadillac in your garage for one hundred dollars." But Prophet Prostitute would be prophesying without her head covered. That is not the Spirit of God operating in their life. The Spirit is nowhere around! Prophet Prostitute needs to have her head shaved, because Prophet Prostitute would be prostituting, selling, and merchandising the gifts of God. She would be prophesying through the woman (the soul), and she will prophesy what you "want" to hear, and not what you "need" to hear. She will seduce you and prostitute the things of God. She will merchandise the gifts of God for her own benefit.

For a man indeed ought not to cover his head (*I Corinthians 1:7*). If my spirit part is praying, I do not need to cover Him. God is doing it. The woman is supposed to be quiet anyway, isn't she? For as much as He, the man, the Spirit, is the image and glory of God.

But the woman would be the glory of the man. The soul is shaped to be the glory or the expression of the spirit if she submits to the spirit. The woman, or bride, is to be a visible expression of an invisible man, or Christ!

For the man is not of the woman, but the woman is of the man. Neither was the man (spirit) created for the woman, but the woman (the soul) was created for the man (spirit). For this cause the woman ought to have authority on her head, or spirit over her head, or covering over her head (mind) because of the angels (*I Corinthians 11:8-10*).

Do you know why the angels are not more visible in our lives today? Because we let the woman pray and speak. The angels are waiting to hear from the man! Nevertheless, neither is the man without the woman, nor the woman without the man, "in" the Lord (*I Corinthians 11:11*).

I think not!! Don't we need the mind of Christ in these things? He says judge "IN" yourselves. Is it seemly that a woman (soul) should pray uncovered? Oh no! Jesus help us!! You know, I went into a church once and they bobby-pinned a paper towel to the top of my head. "Thank you," I said, as I struggled to keep the paper towel on my head.

Then they asked me to take my earrings out of my ears. That took me all day, because I have six holes in my ears. It took me all afternoon to get all those earrings out of my ears! Glory to God! Then they prayed for that demon that made me have my ears pierced to come out.

So you see, I know what I am talking about. That was the woman's voice (the soul) praying over me. That was the woman (soul) prophesying over me. That was the woman (soul) who went and got a piece of paper towel for my head. The woman is SUPPOSED to be quiet in the church. The soul was not supposed to be there praying and leaning to her own natural understanding (*Proverbs 3:5*). Now I ask you, what good did it do me to put a paper towel on my head?!

That is the deceptive wisdom of the woman (soul). *I Corinthians 11:13-14* says, judge yourselves. Does not even nature itself teach you that if a man has long hair, it is a shame unto him? Now you see, we have gotten upset if men have long hair. Long hair (by the spirit) represents the intelligence of a woman (*I Corinthians 11:15*). Now we understand *Revelation 9:7-8:*

> **And the shapes of the locusts were like unto horses prepared unto battle; and on their heads were as it were crowns like gold, and their faces were as the faces of <u>men</u>.**
>
> **And they had hair as the hair of <u>women</u>, and their teeth were as the teeth of lions**.

These soulish messengers with the faces of "men" [they look like they're spiritual, having a "form" of godliness, but denying the power thereof *(II Timothy 3:5)*] have hair as the hair of women and their teeth were as the teeth of lions. Their intelligence and understanding is of the "soul," the woman, their "glory" is soulish, not spiritual and with their teeth they will bite and devour the people of God

> **Be sober, be vigilant; because your adversary the devil, as a roaring "LION," walketh about, seeking whom he may devour.**
>
> *I Peter 5:8*

They are going to merchandise the gifts of the Spirit. They are going to merchandise the anointing of God.

You already see them in the Earth right now. Do you see that in the Church? What do locusts do? They eat fruit, and devour it to the quick; destroying to the root. You do not want to listen to a message from the soul—it will devour your fruit and all that God has made alive within you! It is a soulish message right out of the bottomless pit of religion!

For you may all (does "all" mean "all"?) prophesy one by one that "all" may learn, and all may be comforted. And the spirits of the prophets are subject to the prophets. For God is not the author of confusion, but of peace, as in all churches of the "Saints"— neither male nor female, but saints. Let the women keep "silence" in the churches (*I Corinthians 14:31-34*).

Do not prophesy through that soulish part. Do not prophesy through that woman part. Paul said that you may "all" prophesy, but just don't prophesy through the woman part. He said that now you may "all" prophesy, but just let your "women" (soul) keep silence. I assume that "all" does mean "all," everyone! Doesn't that make sense to you now? Doesn't that bear witness?

Let your women keep silence in the churches: for it is not permitted for them to speak; but they are commanded to be under obedience, as also saith the law (*I Corinthians 14:34*).

Is your woman part under obedience? Is she under obedience to her husband, Christ? She (soul) should be quiet in the church and under obedience. You should have a soulish— woman— part, even if you are a man "physically." But your woman part should be subjected to the husband (Christ). That is why the wife (soul) submits herself to the husband (spirit).

> **And if they (the woman) will learn any thing, let them ask their husbands at home...**
> *I Corinthians 14:35a*

Aren't we to inquire of the spirit, the husband, and not the soul? Let them ask their husbands at home, because it is a shame for a woman to speak in the church. Isn't it a shame to hear a preacher get up and speak (it doesn't matter if it is a male or female, because there is neither male nor female in the Body of Christ) through and by the woman part? It is a shame to hear a message from the soul and not from the Spirit. It is a shame for the bride to speak rather than the Bridegroom. It is a shame for the wife to speak rather than the Husband. It is a shame for the woman to speak rather than the Man! It is a shame for the soul to speak rather than the Spirit!

> **Let all things be done decently and "in order."**
> *I Corinthians 14:40*

CHAPTER NINE

GOD IS NOT INTO MIXTURE!

What does *James 1:8* say? A "double-minded" man is unstable in all his ways. Now let's hear what the Spirit says! Some people say the double-mindedness that James was talking about is doubt and unbelief. But no, double-mindedness is actually a mixture of soul and spirit. The real question you have to ask yourself is, who is controlling your mind? The soul or the spirit? Who is the "head" of "your" house?

If you are allowing the soul to control, the soul is going to eat from the tree of the knowledge of good and evil. If you are allowing the spirit to control, the spirit will eat from the Tree of Life. It will go through the sword, it will go through the message, and it will go through the fire, but it will eat of the Tree of Life. A double-minded man is unstable. *Matthew 6:24* says a man cannot serve two masters. Who are you serving— the soul or the spirit? I like what Jesus said:

Wherefore if thy hand or thy foot offend thee, cut them off, and cast them from thee...

And if thine eye offend thee, pluck it out...
Matthew 18:8a,9a

What was he talking about? If that soulish eye offends you, blind it. Do we walk by faith or by sight? That is what happened to Saul on the Damascus Road (*Acts 9:3*). He was blinded by light from Heaven (the Intelligence of God) and his natural vision (soulish vision) closed down. Ananias had to come and lay hands on him so he could receive his "true" sight and vision through the Spirit of God.

Your soul was never designed to see, she was never designed to speak, and she was never designed to have an intelligence in her own right. She was never designed to pray, she was never designed to prophesy, but she was designed to be quiet, submit herself and give birth! No man can serve two masters; for either he will hate the one, and love the other; or else he will hold to the one, and despise the other (*Matthew 6:24*).

Jesus' instructions were that if the soulish hand is doing something soulish (offensive, contrary to the will of God), cut it off (cease to yield your strength to it). If that soulish foot is walking somewhere it is not supposed to be walking, cut it off (cease to yield your strength to it). If your soulish eye is trying to eat from the tree of the knowledge of good and evil, pluck it out (change your vision)!

It is like Saul after he was on the road to Damascus, where the Bible says he was three days without sight and did neither eat nor drink (Acts 9:9). I submit to you that we have many blind males and females in the Church that can neither eat the bread (His Body) nor drink the water (the Word) because they are blind; they have no sight. They have no spiritual discernment, no revelation, and no vision from God (Revelation 3:18). They are eating from the tree of the knowledge of good and evil, and God is not into mixture.

This is why Jesus prayed for the two blind men sitting by the wayside. Jesus stood still and called them and said, "What will ye that I shall do unto you?" "They" said unto Him, "Lord, that 'our' eyes may be opened." Do you know what Jesus did? He touched their eyes: and immediately their eyes received sight (*Matthew 20:32-34*)! That is why there are "two" blind men by the "wayside" when Jesus comes. The soul and the spirit are both blind and by the wayside (outside the purpose of God). We have to ask Jesus to open our eyes. Why? So that our eyes might "receive sight," not just "see," but receive SIGHT.

If your soul and spirit are blind, do you know who is leading? The blind is leading the blind. And they will both fall into the ditch (*Matthew 15:14*). If you are being led by your soul (the woman), you are definitely ditch-bound. You may as well get the blueprints ready to build a condo in the ditch, because that is where you will be.

Reader, do you have your seat belt on? Good. Let's go deeper into the Spirit. Remember Lot and his wife came out of Sodom and Gomorrah. Lot represents the man (the spirit). Lot's wife represents the soul (the woman). She wants to look back and turn back and remember old wells, old husbands, old moves, the good old days, etc. The Scripture firmly tells us that no man, having put his hand to the plow and looking back, is fit for the kingdom of God.

Can I tell you that before you are going to get anywhere with God, your soul has to be turned to salt? Did He not say we are the salt of the earth? (*Matthew 5:13*). Because your soul (the woman) will always look back, she will always long for what was in Sodom and Gomorrah. As she follows the spirit man out of the old and into the new, she will be turned into salt for seasoning purposes.

I am here to tell you that EVERY experience of my soul (whether good or bad) has "seasoned" my life. And we know that "all" things work "together" for good to them that love God, to them who are the called according to His purpose (*Romans 8:28*). All things, I assume, means ALL THINGS! I can tell you I have learned from my mistakes. Thank God! They have seasoned my life and allowed me to minister to those passing through the same valley of decision.

> **Multitudes, multitudes in the valley of decision: for the day of the Lord is near in the valley of decision.**
> ***Joel 3:14***

We must all stand in the valley of decision at some point, for we are all faced with the same critical decision that must be made, and that is, what shall we do with the Lordship of Jesus Christ? Will we allow our woman (soul) to come into subjection to the Man (Spirit)? <u>We</u> <u>must</u>!! For if a man know not how to rule his <u>own</u> house— <u>temple</u> [What? Know ye not that your body is the <u>temple</u> of the Holy Spirit who is in you, whom ye have of God, and ye are not your own? (I Corinthians 6:19)], how shall he take care of the church of God? I Timothy 3:5.

CHAPTER TEN

TWO MEN IN MY BED!

And as it was in the days of Noe, so shall it also be in the days of the Son of Man.

They did eat, they drank, they married wives, they were given in marriage, until the day that Noe (the man) entered into the ark (the Covenant) and the flood (the water) came, and destroyed them all.
Luke 17:26-27

What does the flood represent to us today? The washing of water by the Word. God said, "Neither shall 'all flesh' be cut off any more by the water of a flood" (*Genesis 9:11*). So what do you suppose God is going to do with the flood today? He is going to "cleanse" all flesh!

Howbeit that was not first which is spiritual, but that which is natural; and afterward that which is spiritual.
I Corinthians 15:46

God cut off all "natural" flesh with a "natural" flood. Today, He will cleanse all flesh with a spiritual flood of His "Living Water."

And it shall come to pass in the last days, saith God, I will pour out of my Spirit upon "ALL FLESH....."
Acts 2:17a

The spirit (Noah— the man) entered the Ark of God, but the soul (ALL FLESH) had to be washed. Likewise also, as it was in the days of Lot; they did eat, they drank, they bought, they sold, they planted, they built; but the same day that Lot went out of Sodom, separated from "all flesh," was the same day that he walked into freedom. At the same time that our spirit (the man) is made free, it will rain fire and brimstone from heaven and destroy or deal with "all flesh." Natural fire destroyed all flesh the first time, but a spiritual fire will deal with all flesh this time (*I Corinthians 15:46*). For our God is a consuming fire (*Hebrews 12:29*). That which is first is natural, and afterward, that which is spiritual.

Even thus shall it be in the day when the Son of man is revealed (*Luke 17:30*). There is a difference between seeing and revealing. There is a difference in the "revealing of" and the "coming of" our Lord.

But as it is written, Eye hath not seen, nor ear heard, neither have entered into the heart of man, the things which God hath prepared for them that love Him.

But God hath revealed them unto us by His Spirit: for the Spirit searcheth all things, yea, the deep things of God.
I Corinthians 2:9-10

That "revealing" is not coming through the soul. The soul does "see." It eats from the tree of the knowledge of good and evil. But what is "revealed" from God comes through the spirit, like the Noah part, the Lot part, the Abraham part, and the man part. The Scripture says, **"In that day, he which shall be upon the housetop, and his stuff in the house, let him not come down to take it away..."** (*Luke 17:31a*). Praise God for a "housetop ministry" in this day, a "caught up" and "raised up" ministry living "in" this world, but not of it!

> **... and he that is in the field, let him likewise not return back.**
> *Luke 17:31b*

Remember Lot's wife.

> **Whosoever shall seek to save his life shall lose it; and whosoever shall lose his life shall preserve it.**
>
> **I tell you, in that night, there shall be two men in one bed; the one shall be taken, and the other shall be left.**
> *Luke 17:33-34*

Some of you may say, "But Sister Connie, I thought that last scripture was talking about the Rapture!" Dear One, if you believe in a rapture, and at the time of this "rapture" there are two men in a bed together, neither one of them are going anywhere! I don't care how you look at it, there is no reason for two men to be in bed together! The Bible says, "Two women shall be grinding together; the one shall be taken and the other left. Two men shall be in the field; the one shall be taken and the other 'left.'" Can I tell you that there "were" two men or two natures in my bed? The man of sin, the "first" man who is of the earth, earthly, and the "second" man who is the Lord of Heaven (*I Corinthians 15:47*). My old self, and the second man, who is Christ. That old man is BEING TAKEN!

The old man of the world, the first man, is being done away with. He is "decreasing," and the new man, who is Christ, is increasing. "He" must increase, but "I" must decrease (*John 3:30*). Therefore, if any man be in Christ, he is a new creature: old things are "passed away"; behold, all things are become new (*II Corinthians 5:17*). That double-minded man is decreasing and I am being renewed in the "spirit" of my mind (*Ephesians 4:23*). There are two women grinding at the mill, but one of them has to be taken (*Luke 17:35*). "My will" must decrease. There are two men working out in the field (the mind) (*Luke 17:35*). One man has to go. The old woman who is the harlot must decrease and the bride must increase. The old mind (field) must be plowed up and renewed. New seeds must be planted to bring harvest to this house. For as a man thinketh in his heart, his mind, so is he (*Proverbs 23:7*).

THE UNNATURAL AFFECTION

He that hath an ear, let him hear what the Spirit is saying to the Church! Let me show you some things about unnatural affection, but by the spirit, not in the natural. Unnatural affection is trying to join the soulish with the soulish. Unnatural affection is a woman lying with another woman. Soul with soul reproduces after the emotion, reproducing after the flesh. Now, if I come and minister spirit to spirit (man to man) but never minister to your hurts (your mind, intellect or emotions), your soul— your woman, then it is unnatural as well, because it is man ministering or joining with man.

We must minister to the whole person. The man (spirit) must minister to the woman (soul). He must always cover her. That is why one of the "men in my bed," the place where God "rests" in me, has to go. One of them has to be thrown out or taken, decreased so that "He" will increase *(John 3:30)*. One of them has to be crucified, for one of them has to die.

> **I am crucified with Christ: nevertheless I live; yet <u>not</u> "I," but "Christ" liveth in me: and the life which I now live in the flesh I live by the faith of the Son of God, who loved me, and gave himself for me.**
>
> *Galatians 2:20*

Jesus said, "For whosoever will save his life, shall lose it; and whosoever will lose his life for my sake shall find it" *(Matthew 16:25)*. In other words, Jesus is saying, "If you are willing to lose 'your' life for My sake; willing to lose that extra one in the bed...the extra one grinding at the mill...lose the extra one out in the field, then, and only then, will you really find 'LIFE.'"

Two of me cannot preach this Word. One of them has to go. Two cannot grind out this wheat. One has to go. Two cannot be in fellowship with the Spirit of God. One of them has to go; one has to be taken. He must increase, but I "must" decrease *(John 3:30)*.

We remember Jesus on the cross, but we have to go to our cross also.

> **That I may know Him, and the power of His resurrection, and the fellowship of His sufferings, being made comformable unto his death...**
>
> *Philippians 3:10*

Think back to the story. How many thieves were beside Jesus on the cross? Two. And there will always be two thieves beside you on your cross. One of them will be your soul, the other will be your old Adam nature. Here, at the cross, we have a picture of the whole man, the soul, the flesh and Jesus as the Spirit. The Word was made flesh and dwelt among us (*John 1:14*). One of the two thieves will always say, "IF thou be Christ" (*Luke 23:39*). That was the soulish part speaking; the part wanting to eat from the tree of the knowledge of good and evil. It may have been dressed as a man, but it was still the woman speaking or leaning to her own understanding. Then the other thief said, "Lord, remember me 'when' thou comest into Thy Kingdom." Jesus said, "Today shalt thou be with me in paradise" (*Luke 23:42-43*). The spirit side, the man side, was at work here. The fallen spirit in the man recognized the need for a Savior. Jesus said, "Today" we will return to paradise, "Today" we will correct what happened in the first paradise, and "Today" you will walk with Me in the cool of the day, unashamed (*Genesis 3:8-10*). The fallen man waited on a "someday." Jesus brought him into Today. I am grieved to say that many Christians walk in a "someday" realm. I hear "Spirit-filled" tongue-talking Christians say, "This way is hard. I am a stranger and a pilgrim in this land." You are not a stranger or a pilgrim in this land!

Now therefore ye are no more strangers and foreigners, but fellow-citizens with the saints, and of the household of God.
Ephesians 2:19

The earth is the Lord's, and the fullness thereof...
Psalms 24:1a

For "<u>evildoers</u>" shall be cut off: but those that wait upon the Lord, <u>they</u> shall <u>inherit</u> the earth.

Psalms 37:9

The Earth is part of "your" inheritance. The two thieves in our life, that "someday" thief and that "if you are" thief, have to be crucified.

Let us reflect on what the Bible says about John the Baptist.

Verily I say unto you, Among them that are born of women there hath not risen a greater than John the Baptist: notwithstanding he that is least in the kingdom of heaven is greater than he.

Matthew 11:11

Do you understand that when John the Baptist was born, no one was born-again? No one's spirit was reconciled. Jesus said John the Baptist was the best that could be born of that soulish realm; that first woman at the mill (*Matthew 24:41*). John the Baptist was born before Christ, under the law. He was born before the crucifixion, and therefore born before the resurrection. He was born from the other woman who had to pass away; the old thoughts and doctrines of religion. He came out of the loins of the wrong priest; he came from an old order. You were born of the loins of Christ, the High Priest.

Verily, I say unto you, among them that are born of women (the soulish realm), there hath not risen a greater than John the Baptist: Notwithstanding, he that is least "in" in the Kingdom of Heaven is greater than he (*Matthew 11:11*).

That is why John the Baptist had to be beheaded (*Luke 9:9*). His authority (his head) was taken because he was not the "fullness" of the man (spirit); he was the forerunner (*Luke 3:15-16*). When he said, "He must increase, but I must decrease" (*John 3:30*), he spoke of his realm, his order, and his authority. His authority had to be taken away so that the Christ, the fullness of the last Adam, could come.

And so it is written, The first man Adam was made a living soul; the last Adam was made a quickening spirit.
I Corinthians 15:45

My dear brothers and sisters, can I tell you that many ministries, many things that we are calling Spiritual, and many things we are calling "Church," are about to be beheaded! Everything that was born of a woman (soul), created after a law of religion, a doctrine or an old order, has got to die! The fullness of time has come, and Jesus Christ is showing "Himself." He is appearing "in" His Church. Before He "comes," He is going to "appear." He is going to be "revealed" before He is "seen." He is going to be glorified "IN" HIS SAINTS. We pray we would be worthy of "this" calling.

When he shall come to be glorified "in" his saints, and to be admired "in" all men that believe...
II Thessalonians 1:10a

We see that the fullness of time has come, for we are seeing the Christ. We are seeing the fullness of "Him." Everything else must decrease!

Church, we must grow up. We must put away childish things. We must quit speaking as children, arguing over our "pet" doctrines. We must quit thinking like children, and allow the spirit of our minds to be renewed. We must quit understanding as children with our "someday it'll be worth it all" mentality (*I Corinthians 13:11*). He must increase and we must decrease (John 3:30). We must not have "unnatural affection" for the "good old days." We must not mourn for Saul; his day is over (*I Samuel 16:1*). This is a new day! We must grab hold of the plow and not look back.

And Jesus said unto him, No man, having put his hand to the plough, and looking back, is fit for the kingdom of God.
Luke 9:62

CHAPTER ELEVEN

A WORD TO "THE DEAD"

Now, let's go into the deep of God! In *I Thessalonians* Chapter 4, we see a "dead" person's message—it is not for everyone. This is not for the woman. This is not going to feed the soulish part. If your woman starts talking and acting up, you are going to have to tell her to be quiet. That woman is always going to want to eat from the tree of knowledge of good and evil. You are going to have to say, "Woman, be quiet." Be silent, you are going to have to learn to be under subjection, to your husband, the spirit, the Christ!

But I would not have you to be ignorant, brethren, concerning them which are asleep, that ye sorrow not, even as others which have no hope.

For if we believe that Jesus died and rose again, even so them also which sleep in Jesus will God bring with him.

For this we say unto you by the word of the Lord, that we which are alive and remain unto the coming of the Lord shall not prevent them which are asleep.

For the Lord himself shall descend from heaven with a shout, with the voice of the archangel, and with the trump of God: and the dead in Christ shall rise first:

Then we which are alive and remain shall be caught up together with them in the clouds, to meet the Lord in the air: and so shall we ever be with the Lord.

I Thessalonians 4:13-17

Our only problem is that He is talking about those who are asleep and those who are dead. My Grandmama is asleep; she joined that great cloud of witnesses eight years ago (*Hebrews 12:1*); however, I am dead in Him.

I am Crucified with Christ: nevertheless I live, yet "not" I, but Christ liveth in me: by the faith of the Son of God, who loved me and gave himself for me.

Galatians 2:20

Know ye not, that so many of us as were baptized into Jesus Christ were baptized into his death?

Therefore we are buried with him by baptism into death: that like as Christ was raised up from the dead by the glory of the Father, even so we also should walk in newness of life.

For if we have been planted together in the likeness of his death, we shall be also in the likeness of his resurrection:

Knowing this, that our old man is crucified with him, that the body of sin might be destroyed, that henceforth we should not serve sin.

For he that is dead is freed from sin.

Romans 6:3-7

That I may know him, and the power of his resurrection, and the fellowship of his sufferings, being made conformable unto his death.

Philippians 3:10

Jesus is going to bring the sleeping with Him, but there is going to be a dead group "IN" Him. They will eat His flesh and drink His blood. They will have that woman (soul) silent. He is raising up a remnant among us that have the soulish part under subjection to the Spirit! A people eating from the Tree of Life, that have been through the sword, that have been through the fire, that have been through the message, and that are swallowed up in Him! They're "dead" in Him; "dead" to their desires, their wants, and even their own needs. They are denying themselves!

> **Then said Jesus unto his disciples, If any man will come after me, let him deny himself, and take up his cross, and follow me.**
>
> **For whosoever will save his life shall lose it: and whosoever will lose his life for my sake shall find it.**
> *Matthew 16:24-25*

He is about to "raise" up a people! You know why He is raising them up? So the world can see them! So He can present "Himself!" He is going to raise them up out of doctrine and He is going to raise them up out of tradition. They will hear the sound of the trumpets. Do you know who the trumpets are? The trumpets are His Prophets!

The Trumpets are those that declare the Word of the Lord. There are seven trumpets (*Revelation 8:2*). Seven means fullness; the completeness of God. *I Corinthians 15:52* says, "at the last trump" there are going to be some dead people who are going to be "raised" up. Hear me by the Spirit! There are some dead people in the earth! They are dead unto themselves! They are dead! God says, "I am going to raise them up in the last day incorruptible and changed!" We will recognize them! They will be "raised up" "out" of doctrine, "out" of tradition, "out" of religion, "out" of the soulish, and caught up into Him! Praise God!

These are they who are not going to eat from the tree of the knowledge of good and evil, but they are going to eat from the Tree of Life, Christ Himself! We will see them. He is raising them up! There is always going to be a people that will be alive, but they are going to "remain." They do not want to walk in the high places of God. They are not going to come out. They are not going to be a separate people. They love Egypt! They just want to die and go to heaven. They are alive, but remain in "that old-time religion." They want their "mansion of glory" rather than "becoming" a mansion, a house, for His Glory! They're ready to give the earth to the devil— destroy everything, torture everybody who does not fit their idea of being "worthy"—and be raptured out of here! If only they would be like father Abraham, who petitioned God "not" to destroy Sodom and Gomorrah (*Genesis 18:24-33*). Abraham had a vision of *Revelation 11:15*!

> **And the seventh angel sounded; and there were great voices in heaven, saying, The kingdoms of this world are become the kingdoms of our Lord, and of his Christ; and he shall reign for ever and ever.**
>
> ***Revelation 11:15***

There is a people that are coming up on Mount Zion. Obadiah and Nehemiah call them saviors and deliverers. They are going to come "up" on Mount Zion (*Nehemiah 9:27, Obadiah 1:21*).

> **But ye are come unto mount Sion, and unto the city of the living God, the heavenly Jerusalem, and to an innumerable company of angels,**
>
> **To the general assembly and church of the firstborn, which are written in heaven, and to God the Judge of all, and to the "spirits" of just "men" made perfect,**
> **And to Jesus the mediator of the new covenant, and to the blood of sprinkling, that speaketh better things than that of Abel.**
>
> *Hebrews 12:22-24*

Can I say this another way? Suffer not the woman, the Church, to teach nor to usurp authority over the man (Christ). Have the woman learn in silence. Let her be dead in Him. Therefore, allow Him to "raise" you up. You cannot be raised up if you are not dead. When Jesus yielded up the ghost, the rocks were rent and the graves were open.

> **And behold, the veil of the temple was rent in twain from the top to the bottom; and the earth did quake, and the rocks rent;**
>
> **And the graves were opened; and many bodies of the saints which slept arose.**
>
> *Matthew 27:51-52*

Do you know that Jesus is "resurrecting" in His Church? We are not only knowing Him, but He is being revealed to us. As He is being revealed to us and in us, every other rock is splitting, every denomination is splitting and every other rock that is a substitute for Him is splitting. For He is the only true Rock! There are people coming up out of their graves. What does the grave represent? What are you made of? The dust, the earth (*I Corinthians 15:547*). I have already come up out of my grave, because it is not me who lives any more, it is He. I have left the earthly man and am now a partaker of the heavenly man (Christ).

Every rock in my life is being split, and I am coming up out of this grave. I have been redeemed from spiritual death. I am no longer in hell, the place of the lost and separated. I am now seated with Him! (*Ephesians 2:6*) We cannot reproduce life after God if we are carnally minded. For to be carnally minded "is" death; but to be spiritually minded is life and peace (*Romans 8:6*). We must come to the temple like Hannah and let the priest, Christ, speak life into our womb (*I Samuel 1:17*).

Why not pray this prayer along with me?

We thank you, Father. We thank You for bringing clarity, understanding and divine wisdom to us. We thank You, Lord, that we have heard from Your very Mind, from Your very ways, from Your very thoughts. Father, we thank You for Your Word. We thank You for Your anointing. We say thank You for ever making us mindful of that woman, that soul, that desire to speak out and usurp authority. Father, help us to be mindful of her. Oh Father, we have seen the woman's ministry, and the woman is just like the great harlot. The woman that sits upon many waters. She tells us all the things we want to hear. She tells us we do not have to make sacrifices and that we do not have to pay a price. That is the woman speaking; the soulish part speaking. Father, help us to vomit out all the fruit from the tree of the knowledge of good and evil. We want to be filled with the fruit from the Tree of Life. Help "restore" that soulish part, that woman part, that she might submit herself. Help us to bring her under her covering, which is the Spirit of Christ, the Man, so that the spirit would overshadow her, cover her, so that she may not speak through the Body of Christ any more! We pray that the Man, the Husband, the Bridegroom, will be elevated and take his rightful position in the land! And we decree and declare Revelation 11:15, that as the seventh angel sounds—great voices are declaring from the heavens that "the kingdoms of this world are become the kingdom of our Lord and of His Christ; and He shall reign for ever and ever." AMEN!

CONCLUSION

GOD'S ORDER IN EARTH AS IT IS IN HEAVEN

I am in no way doing away with God's "natural" structure in the home and family. God has an order in the home, just as He does in the Church, which is to be honored and obeyed. Thy kingdom come, thy will be done in "earth" as it "is" in heaven (*Matthew 6:10*).

- Christ (the man) the Head of the Church (the woman)

- The husband (the man) as the head of the wife (the woman) *Ephesians 5:23*

- The wife submitted, nourished and cherished and loved (*Ephesians 5:22, 25-26*)

- The husband reverenced by the wife (*Ephesians 5:33*)

- The children obeying their parents (*Ephesians 6:1*)

What I have hoped to do in this book is explain the "great mystery" concerning "Christ and the Church" (*Ephesians 5:32*) by showing Christ as the Man, the Bridegroom, and the Spirit, and by showing the Church as the woman, the bride, and the soul. David had a revelation in *Psalms 34:2*, when he said, "My soul shall make 'her' boast to the Lord." It is time for us to look "into" God's Word. This is a serious hour, and we cannot afford to argue over petty doctrine while God's people are destroyed every day for lack of knowledge (*Hosea 4:6*).

It is my intention not to offend, but to encourage other women in ministry, who have been oppressed while knowing the call of God was upon them. It is also my hope that men will read this book and be free to allow women in ministry to move in their proper place. My dear, dear brothers, we do not want to compete with you, but we want to complement you.

This is such a wonderful day! The harvest is plenteous, but the laborers are so few. God is sending the laborers into His vineyard, regardless of their gender. Let us encourage one another, let us uplift His Name, and let the man (Christ) be exalted. Amen!!

To request a complete listing of books, tapes and other materials or itinerary of Dr. Connie Williams, or to contact her for speaking engagements, conferences, seminars or crusades, please write or call her:

Dr. Connie Williams
Connie Williams Ministries International
P.O. Box 250
Ball Ground, Georgia 30107
USA
1-(770) 735-4554